# HELPFUL
# HOME HINTS

# HELPFUL HOME HINTS

## Linda Hall & Diane Webber

### Pine Candle Adult New Reader's Series

PINE
CANDLE

Copyright 1991 by Alberta Association for Adult Literacy

Printed in Canada

First printed in 1991  5 4 3 2 1

The publisher:
*Lone Pine Publishing*
206, 10426-81 Avenue
Edmonton, Alberta, Canada
T6E 1X5

Canadian Cataloguing in Publication Data
Webber, Diane.
  Helpful home hints

ISBN 1-55105-006-4
  1. Readers for new literates. 2. English language — Textbooks for second language learners.
3. Readers (Adult) 4. Home economics. I. Hall, Linda 1950- II. Title.
PE1126.N43W45 1991   428.6'2   C91-091630-6

Cover illustration: *Horst H. Krause*
Illustrations: *Cam Wilson*
Editorial: *Lloyd Dick*
Printing: *Kromar Printing Ltd., Winnipeg, Manitoba, Canada*

*The revision of this publication was made possible by a grant from the Secretary of State for the International Literacy Year (1990).*

The publisher gratefully acknowledges the assistance of the Federal Department of Communications, Alberta Culture and Multiculturalism, the Canada Council, and the Alberta Foundation for the Arts in the production of this book

# CONTENTS

# THE LAST TEN YEARS

Finding suitable and enjoyable reading material for adults reading at basic levels has always been a problem. In 1980, literacy instructors at Lakeland College in northern Alberta decided to produce the books they needed themselves. Literacy instructor Colleen Hanley received a summer STEP grant and hired two people, Diane Webber and Terri Fuglem, who wrote and illustrated the original 13 booklets over two summers. The ideas for the booklets came out of brainstorming sessions between Colleen, Terri and Diane. "I had a pretty good idea of my student's interests," said Colleen.

Copies were sold to and used by numerous literacy programs throughout Alberta. In 1984, the Alberta Association for Adult Literacy took over the copyright. Colleen, an AAAL board member at the time, felt that a provincial literacy association would be better than a college at selling books.

In 1990, the AAAL received an International Literacy Year grant to revise, rewrite and upgrade the six most popular booklets in the series. Literacy instructors and students were polled as to their favourites. Linda Hall was hired as editor for the AAAL. Lone Pine Publishing was contracted to edit, produce and market the new books. A lot of research, revising and updating was done.

The Pine Candle Adult New Reader's Series is the result. With the co-operation of Lone Pine Publishing, we have produced a series of six books that can be read and enjoyed by the "adult new reader." But many other people should also find them enjoyable, useful and informative.

There are six books in the Pine Candle Adult New Reader's Series:

Alberta Highlights
Helpful Home Hints
Hockey: Canada's National Game
Night Skies
Rodeo West
Souped Up

# FAMILY GROOMING
## FOR EVERYONE

*CHAPPED HANDS*

Your hands are badly chapped from hard work. What do you do? Cover them with petroleum jelly. Then put on clean cotton gloves. Keep the gloves on for an hour, or overnight. Your hands will be soft again!

*WHO NEEDS SHAMPOO?*

Does the thought of shampoo make you weak, yet greasy hair is driving you crazy? Try this: push an old, clean pair of pantyhose over your hair brush. Now brush your hair. The nylon will pick up oil from your hair.

**or**

Brush a pinch of baby powder through your hair.

*DRY SKIN BATH*

Mix 1/2 cup of instant non-fat dry milk into your bath. Your skin will love it. It costs just pennies.

*OUT OF TOOTHPASTE?*

Baking soda works just great! Wet your toothbrush. Then place a large dab of baking soda on it. Brush away.

### DOG BATH

When there's no time to give your dog a bath, sprinkle some baking soda into its coat. Then brush it out.

### SUNBURN PAIN

Do you need to soak away sunburn pain? Try two cups of milk in a cool bath,

**or**

pour some baking soda into a cool bath.

### SUN AND WIND CHAPPED FACE

If a day of skiing has left your face red and sore, try this. Soak some cotton balls in vinegar. Now dab these on your face.

## FOR THE WOMAN OF THE HOUSE

### HAIR CONDITIONER

Mix 1 part white vinegar with 7 parts water. Pour this through your hair after you shampoo. Your hair will gleam.

### DRY, DAMAGED HAIR

Massage some mayonnaise through your hair. Leave this on for 30 minutes. Then shampoo and rinse well.

### SHINY NAILS

Rub vinegar on your nails before you polish them. Your nails will look shinier. And they won't chip so easily.

## BROKEN LIPSTICK

Heat the broken ends with a match. Press them back together. Now cool the lipstick in the fridge.

## LIP GLOSS

Use petroleum jelly on your lips for a new look. You can use it on your eyelashes and eyebrows, too.

## PUFFY EYELIDS, SORE EYES

Do you have a potato, a cucumber, or a couple of used damp tea bags? Grate the potato. Put the pieces on your closed eyelids. Or, slice the cucumber and place the pieces on your closed eyelids. Or, put the used tea bags on your eyelids. Then put damp cotton balls on them and lie back for 20 minutes. The puffiness will disappear.

## PERFUMED BATH OIL

Going out on the town? Cover yourself in fragrance. Add a few drops of perfume and one cap of baby oil to your bath.

## MOISTURIZERS

When your bottle of face moisturizer is low, add an ounce of water for each ounce of remaining moisturizer. Mix well before using.

## SKIN TONER

When you are using a cotton ball to apply skin toner, don't saturate the ball with toner. Soak the cotton ball with water first, then apply the toner. You will save money this way by making your toner last longer.

These facials cost just pennies: For **oily skin,** mix about 1/8 cup of finely ground oatmeal with a little bit of water or witch hazel until it becomes a thick paste. Now spread this on your face. Leave it on for about 20 minutes. Then rinse it off.

For **dry skin** mix a bit of honey with an egg yolk. Spread this on your face. Leave it on for about 20 minutes and then rinse it off.

For **large pores or wrinkles** beat 1 egg white until it becomes a meringue. Apply this all over your face. Let it harden. Then rinse it off with cool water.

*FACIAL TONER*

Use witch hazel. It's much cheaper than commercial toners. It's also gentler than alcohol. It won't dry your skin. You can buy witch hazel in your drug store.

*MAKE-UP REMOVER*

Olive oil works well. Just dab on and tissue off. Olive oil also makes a good moisturizer for your face.

# BABY CARE
## BRINGING UP BABY

Home is where your baby is safe—or should be. But there are more dangers in your home than you may think. Here are some ways to keep your baby safe:

- Do not tie or harness your baby into the crib at night. Your baby could turn over and strangle on the ties.

- Don't let a baby sleep or nap on a water bed.

- Place your baby's high chair so that their little legs cannot reach anything. Children can push against nearby walls or furniture and fall over.

- Here's a way to keep baby's high chair secure: buy a large screen door hook and eye. Screw the hook onto the back of the chair. Now screw the eye into the wall. When your baby is in the chair, hook the chair to the wall and always fasten the chair's seat belt.

- Playpens are nice to have. You can work out in the garden, or just sit out in the sun and your baby is safe. But there are some things you should know:

Playpen sides should be made of fine mesh. Some older playpens have walls made with mesh with large holes. These sometimes cause injury when baby's buttons got caught in the mesh.

Do not put large toys in the playpen. A child might use them to climb out.

- Babies must be in car seats while travelling. Car seats come in many different sizes. Make sure yours is the right size for your child. Also make sure that your baby's seat has been approved by the motor vehicle safety standards set up by Transport Canada. Always remember to fasten the seat belt before you drive away.

- A lot of parents like to carry their babies around in moulded plastic baby carriers. These are quite handy. But these are not car seats. Don't use them in cars or trucks. Always remember to fasten the safety belt on the baby in a carrier.

## DIAPERING YOUR BABY

Should you use cloth diapers, disposables, or a diaper service?

*DISPOSABLE DIAPERS*

Disposable diapers are easy to use, but they may cause environmental problems. More than 2 million used disposable diapers are put into Canadian landfills each year. The plastic backsheets on these diapers take a very long time to break down in landfills. It may take 500 years for them to become part of the soil again.

If you wish to use disposable diapers, look for the new "biodegradable" types. They break down into the environment faster than regular diapers. Also, be sure to rinse off messy diapers into your toilet before throwing them away. If messy diapers are not rinsed off before they are put in the garbage, they can cause disease to spread.

*CLOTH DIAPERS*

A diaper service is convenient. You use cloth diapers, yet you don't have to wash them yourself. A diaper service will pick them up and wash them for you. Then they deliver clean ones to your home. Diaper services are usually available only in larger towns and cities. Look in your yellow pages under Diaper Service to see if your area has one. Your other choice is washing cloth diapers yourself.

*COSTS*

A 1987 survey which compared costs of cloth diapers and disposable diapers found that cloth diapers cost a lot less. The survey found that it would cost $500 – $950 for 2 1/2 years to use cloth diapers. This includes the cost of laundry detergent and running the washing machine. The survey found that using disposable diapers would cost between $2,000 – $2,300. By comparison, a diaper service cost between $1,000 – $1,200.

Don't worry about sticking your baby with pins. Some cloth diapers now come with Velcro fasteners.

Washing diapers doesn't need to be a headache. First, put used diapers in a pail about 3/4 filled with water. Add about 3/4 cup of vinegar to the water. Rinse out messy diapers in the toilet before you put them in the pail.

To wash them, dump the whole diaper pail into the washing machine. Then let it spin out. Now add detergent and start a full cycle. Use hot water. It's also a good idea to run an extra rinse at the end. Don't use a fabric softener. If you do, the diapers could become less absorbent.

Every year thousands of poisonings are reported to poison control centres in Alberta. These accidents are preventable. Here are some ways to poison proof your home:

- Keep the telephone number of your doctor, the ambulance, the poison control centre, and the fire department right next to the telephone. The telephone number for the **Alberta Poison Centre is 1-800-332-1414.** This is a free call from anywhere in Alberta.

- When you buy pills and medicines, ask for child resistant containers.
- Never tell your children that medicine is candy.

- Always replace the cap before you put a medicine bottle down, even if it's just for a second.

- Use safety latches on cupboards and drawers.

- Teach your children about poisons.

- Keep cleaners and other poisonous liquids in their original containers. If you pour liquids into another container, you may not remember what the liquid was.

If you mix your own cleaning products (like the window washer recipe found in this book), make sure you label it. Use a permanent marking pen to write down what the contents are. Write on the container itself, on a label, or on a piece of tape.

- Store household cleaners and other poisonous materials in a high cupboard — the shelf above your broom closet is a good place — instead of under the kitchen sink.

- Don't leave plastic bags lying around.

- Some of your house plants may be poisonous. Keep these plants on high shelves away from children's curious fingers. Here are the names of some poisonous plants: philodendron, dieffenbachia, and mistletoe. Here are the names of some garden plants which are poisonous: tomato leaves and vines, rhubarb leaves, and new shoots on potato plants. If you have a plant which you don't know about, call your nearest Alberta Agriculture office, or horticulture centre.

*BEDTIME STORIES*

Do you travel a lot? Are you away a lot in the evenings? Record your children's favourite bedtime stories on cassette. Then have your baby-sitter play them for your children. Now they can listen to your voice anytime.

*TREASURE HUNT GAME*

Here is a good birthday party game. Hide a "treasure" that a child might like in your yard or house. This could be a candy bar or a little toy. The children can search for it by reading clues. Write some clues in code. Write some in invisible ink. Write others in erasable ink.

Lemon juice makes good invisible ink. Dip a fine brush into it. Write on plain white paper. You will not see the words. Now hold it over a candle. The heat from the candle will make the words appear like magic.

To make the hunt harder, write some clues in erasable ink. Erasable ink is blue-black. It looks fine on paper. Yet it just wipes off. The first child to see this clue can wipe it clean.

The recipe for erasable ink is in this book. It is in the section called "Recipes."

*POOL MONEY*

Are your children always at the pool or the beach? Sew small cloth pockets on their beach towels. You can cut up an old towel for this purpose. Fasten these pockets with Velcro. The pockets will hold pool passes, snack money, or other valuables.

*FAMILY COUPONS*

Have your children think of six things they would like to do as a family. Going to the zoo, swimming, or baking a cake together are a few ideas. You can do the same. Then put the ideas into a jar. Take turns choosing a coupon and doing the things listed there.

*SICK CHILD*

Put together a small box of craft projects that your child can work on. The box could hold things like tape, scissors, felt, yarn, and glue.

## CHRISTMAS IDEAS

*PLACE MATS*

Save your old Christmas cards. Children can make Christmas place mats out of them. Have them cut out pictures from the old cards and paste them onto sheets of construction paper. You may wish to take these to a printing shop and get them laminated. Then they will last longer and will wipe clean.

The pictures from old Christmas cards also make good tree ornaments or window decorations. Your children can cut out the pictures they like. Then punch a hole at the top of each cutout. Use yarn, ribbon, or a twist tie to hang them onto the tree.

*GIFT TAGS*

Why spend money on gift tags when you can make your own? Children will enjoy helping to make these gift tags. Cut out rectangles from red or green sheets of construction paper. Fold them in half, lengthwise. Then cut out small pictures from old Christmas cards. Paste these onto the front of the folded pieces. Now, write your messages on the inside of the cards. Then attach them to your gifts.

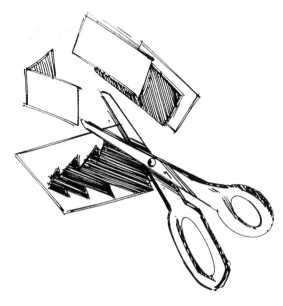

Here's a Christmas gift that children can make. It will be used all year! You will need:

- a small calendar for the coming year
- 12 sheets of construction paper
- paints, felt, or coloured pencils and paper

Have your child draw or paint a picture for each month of the year. Glue each picture and the monthly calendar to a sheet of construction paper. Now put the pages in order and punch two holes at the top. Then tie them together with ribbon.

Did you know that you can make paste, paint, and even playdough? It's much cheaper than buying it. Here's how:

### • Playdough •
1 cup salt
1 1/2 cups flour
1/2 cup water
2 tbsp. vegetable oil
A few drops of food colouring
*Mix all the ingredients together. Store this in the fridge in a plastic bag. It will keep for a long time.*

### • Paste •
Put a handful of flour into a bowl. Add water a little at a time until the mixture is sticky. It should be quite thick. This works on paper, and is a lot cheaper than white glue. It also won't stain clothes. It isn't poisonous either.

### • Erasable Ink•
Mix:
12 drops of iodine
3 tsp. of water
1 tsp. of corn starch
*Use a fine brush to write with this ink.*

### • Soap flake paint •
Mix a little water with soap flakes (not detergent). Ivory Flakes work well. Divide the mixture into jars

or cups. Add food colouring to each jar. Now your child is ready to paint pictures.

### • Finger paint •

Mix equal parts of flour and salt with a little water to make a paste. Divide the paste and put it into jars or cups. Add food colouring to each jar. Cover your children's clothes with aprons or old towels. Spread newspapers on the table and put then sheets of white paper on top. Now let your children dip their fingers in the jars and paint away.

### • Clay •

Mix one cup flour, one cup salt, and enough water to make a very stiff dough. Children can make their creations, paint them, and then let them harden. But, be careful. This kind of clay breaks easily when it dries.

# YOUR CHILDCARE TIPS

# COMING CLEAN
## SHORT CUTS

*ALUMINUM POTS*

Put one part vinegar and four parts water in the stained pot. Let this simmer on the stove until the stain disappears,

*BRASS CLEANERS*

Mix equal quantities of salt and flour. Add enough vinegar to make a paste Brush this on tarnished brass and let it stand a few minutes. Then rinse it off,

**or**

rub toothpaste on the brass. Small scratches will vanish.

*COPPER CLEANERS*

Mix equal parts of salt and flour. Add vinegar to make a paste. Coat the copper. Let it dry. Wash it off with warm, soapy water. Then dry it with a soft cloth,

**or**

dissolve three tablespoons of salt in about a cup of vinegar. Put this in an old spray bottle. Spray it on the copper. Leave it on for one hour. Wipe it off.

*SUBSTITUTE SILVER POLISH*

Try rubbing a little bit of toothpaste on the silver with a soft cloth.

## KEEP THAT SILVER SHINY

Get a piece a white chalk. Store it with your silver. Your polishing days are practically over.

## SPARKLING DISHES

Squeeze a bit of lemon juice into your dish water. The acid from the lemon will cut the grease in the dishwater.

## STREAKY WINDOWS

Clean them with a solution of half white vinegar and half water,

**or**

a mixture of 1/4 cup ammonia and two cups of water. Wipe windows with clean dry cloths, paper towels, or crumpled newspapers.

## WINDOW WASHER

Try this recipe which comes from the *Canadian Consumer Magazine:*
Mix:
2/3 cup of methyl alcohol (available in drug stores)
1 teaspoon of liquid detergent
4 cups of water
*Seal this tightly in a big jar. Put what you need in an old spray bottle.*

## EASY OVEN CLEANING

Put a bowl of ammonia in your oven. Leave it in overnight. Take it out in the morning. Now spray the oven with oven cleaner or with a mixture of water and baking soda. It will wipe clean!

Before those greasy stains have a chance to "set" in your oven, pour salt on them. Wait three minutes. Then wipe them clean.

### ARE YOUR POTS AND YOUR ELECTRIC FRYING PAN GRIMY WITH GREASE?

Put on rubber gloves. Now coat your pots with ammonia. Cover them tightly with plastic bags and leave over night. Next morning, rinse your pots under the tap with warm water. They will shine like new!

### SAFETY TIPS FOR WORKING WITH AMMONIA

• Always use rubber gloves.
• Avoid breathing it in. Keep a window open when you are using it.
• *Never* mix ammonia with bleach. That combination is very dangerous.

### CLOSET MILDEW

Store a barbecue coal in each corner of your closet. That mildew smell will be gone forever.

### DULL TILES

Wash the floor. Now put 1/2 cup of sour milk in your rinse water. It adds a gloss to the floor.

### FURNITURE POLISH

Here's an environmentally friendly polish for your furniture. Mix one part lemon juice and two parts of olive oil or vegetable oil,

**or**

mix one tablespoon carnauba wax and two cups of mineral oil. Place this in the top of a double boiler. When it cools you have an environmentally friendly furniture polish. You can buy carnauba wax in most hobby stores. You can buy mineral oil in a drug store.

## STAINS, STAINS, AND MORE STAINS

The best way to get rid of stains is to keep them from happening in the first place! Put place mats at the front and back doors. Use coasters for drinks. Line your drawers with waterproof paper. Don't carry pens or lipstick around in your pockets.

*ALCOHOLIC BEVERAGES*

Sponge the stain with cold water. Pour a little liquid laundry detergent onto the stain or make a paste or powdered laundry detergent and water. Let it sit for a few minutes then wash as usual.

*BLOOD (FRESH)*

Soak the stain in cold water for 30 minutes. Then wash the fabric with cool, soapy water. If the stain is still there, place a few drops of ammonia on the stain. Then rub it with soap and rinse.

*BLOOD (OLD)*

Apply a few drops of ammonia. Then wash the fabric in warm, soapy water.

*BUTTER*

Wash it out with warm, soapy water.

*CANDLE WAX*

Harden the wax with ice to harden it. Scrape off as much as you can. Cover the spot with a folded paper towel. Iron it. The wax should stick to the paper towel.

*CAR GREASE*

Scrape off as much grease as you can. Rub lard or a mixture of soap and baking soda on the stain. Then wash with warm, soapy water.

---

*THE THREE "P'S" IN STAIN REMOVAL*

### • Promptness
It's a race against time when you are faced with a stain. Old stains, or stains on clothing which have already gone through a washing machine, may be impossible to get out. Never try to get a stain out with hot water. Hot water sometimes will "set" a stain.

### • Patience
If the item is worth saving, then it is worth the time to try to get the stain out. You might have to try many different products.

### • Perseverance
You may have to try to remove the stain many times before it comes

---

### CHEWING GUM

Rub the area with ice to harden it. Then scrape away as much gum as possible. Then, saturate the area with dry-cleaning solvent. Repeat if you need to. Let the fabric dry between treatments. If a sugar stain remains after the gum is removed, sponge it with a little soapy water.

### CHOCOLATE OR COFFEE

Soak the stain in cool water. Now sponge it with soap and borax. Then wash it in hot water.

### DEODORANT

Sponge the stain in warm, soapy water. Rinse. Then dry. If the stain is still there, try again.

### EGG

Soak in cold water. Then wash in warm, sudsy water. Never use hot water.

### FRUIT AND FRUIT JUICE

Stretch the spot over a bowl. Pour boiling water through it from about two feet up. This may sound strange, but it really works!

### GRASS

Rub the stain with glycerine. You can buy glycerine in your drug store. Wait for 30 minutes. Then wash with warm, soapy water.

### GRAVY

Sponge with cool water. Work liquid detergent into the stain. Rinse.

### INK (BALLPOINT)

Spray hair spray on the stain, then rub it with a clean, dry cloth,

**or**

apply nail polish remover. When the stain starts to blur, sponge with water. Rinse thoroughly,

**or**

wet fabric with cold water. Apply a paste of lemon juice and cream of tartar. Let it sit for an hour. Then wash it as usual.

### INK (FELT PEN)

Smear a bit of toothpaste on the stain. Rub it in and then rinse with clear water,

**or**

try nail polish remover or rubbing alcohol. Sponge with water and then rinse.

## ICE CREAM

Soak in cold water before washing.

## KETCHUP

Sponge the stain with cool water. Then soak it in cold water. Leave it for 30 minutes. Then wash it as usual.

## LIME DEPOSITS IN DISHWASHER

Gently pour 1/2 cup of liquid bleach into the bottom of the machine. Let it run through the first wash. After this drains, add two cups of vinegar. Rinse, but don't let it run through the dry cycle. To keep your dishwasher fresh, add 1/2 cup of vinegar to the rinse cycle each week.

## LIME DEPOSITS IN TOILET BOWL

Put one cup of vinegar and 1/8 cup muriatic acid in the toilet bowl. Let this mixture become foamy. Then scrub the bowl and rinse. You can buy muriatic acid in a drug store.

## MILDEW

Wash the fabric in hot, sudsy water. Then dab it with a bit of lemon juice and a pinch of salt. Dry it in the sun.

## MUSTARD

Brush off any dry mustard. Work liquid detergent into the stain. Let the fabric soak over night. Then wash in hot water.

*PAINT - NEW (LATEX/WATER BASED)*

Rinse in warm water while the stains are still wet.

*PAINT - OLD (LATEX/WATER BASED)*

Rub petroleum jelly into the stain. That will make it soft. Now sponge it with turpentine and wash it in warm, sudsy water.

*PAINT (OIL-BASED)*

Read the directions for thinning, and use that thinner to remove the paint.

*RUST*

Rub the stain with salt. Then saturate the stain with lemon juice. Dry the fabric in the sun. Then wash as usual.

*SINKS, KEEP THEM CLEAN*

Is your stainless steel sink rusting? Take a raw potato, and rub it in scouring powder. Then rub it on the rust and watch the stains vanish!

**or**

mix boiling water with 1/4 cup baking soda and two ounces of vinegar. Pour this into your sink. Then wipe gently.

*SCORCH MARKS ON GLASS BAKING BOWLS*

Mix two teaspoons of cream of tartar in one quart of boiling water. Let this mixture stand five minutes.

*WHITE WATER RINGS ON WOOD*

Rub toothpaste into the rings. Use a soft cloth. Rub it firmly into the wood.

*WINE OR FRUIT STAINS ON THE RUG*

Cover the stain with salt and let the salt absorb the liquid. Then vacuum up the salt. If part of the stain is left, sponge it with vinegar and water. Be careful not to saturate the carpet.

*WINE (RED)*

Sprinkle salt on the stain. Then dip the fabric into cold water.

*WINE (WHITE)*

Stretch the fabric over a bowl. Pour boiling water through it from about 2 feet above.

*URINE*

Sponge the stain with ammonia. Then wash it in warm water.

**CALL YOUR DISTRICT HOME ECONOMIST IF YOU NEED HELP IN REMOVING A REALLY STUBBORN STAIN!**

# FIX IT FAST

*DENTS IN WOOD FURNITURE*

Place a damp cloth on the dent. Now hold a hot iron over it. The wood will swell back into place.

*BURNS IN WOOD*

Try clear nail polish remover. Use a cotton swab to rub it very carefully into the burn. Is there still a mark there? Then get a dull knife. Scrape the burn gently. Scrape until all the traces of the burn are gone. Now smooth some clear nail polish into the hole, in layers. Remember, each layer must be dry before the next one is applied. Then you can use furniture polish to give the wood a nice finish.

*ONE STEP AT A TIME*

How can you paint the steps and still get into your house? Do the job in two stages. On the first day paint every other step. Let that dry. On the next day paint the ones you missed. You can still use the stairs this way.

*LOOSE FLOOR TILES*

Cover the loose tiles with aluminum foil. Then rub a hot iron over them. This will soften any old glue remaining under the tiles. Use some heavy books to flatten the tiles until the glue hardens.

## CIGARETTE BURNS ON THE CARPET

First, trim off the burned yarns. Then get some carpet fuzz from near the baseboard. You will need a few rug strands, too. Clip a few from under chairs or couches, where the missing strands won't be noticed. Put some clear glue into the burn hole. Fill it with the fuzz and yarns. Cover it with a strip of foil. Put some paper towels on top of this. Then put a book on top until the glue dries.

## ROVING FURNITURE

Do you have a sectional couch? Is it always drifting apart? Put screen door hook and eyes on the back legs, then hook them together.

## SWEATING PIPES

This happens when cold water in the pipes condenses on the outside of plumbing pipes. You can fix the problem by wrapping insulation around the pipes. You can buy special pipe insulation at a hardware store. Make sure that the pipe is dry before you try to wrap it.

## LEAKY PIPES

Leaky pipes should be replaced as soon as possible, but you can temporarily stop the leak by wrapping the pipe with electrical tape. Shut off the water valve, dry the pipes, and tape up the leaks.

## PLUGGED DRAINS

If you notice that your sink or tub is draining slowly, don't ignore it. Pour kettles of boiling water down the drain. Sometimes, this is all it takes to clear the drain.

If that doesn't work, use a commercial drain cleaner. Follow the directions carefully. Don't pour drain cleaner into a sink filled with water — you could end up with an even worse problem.

To drain standing water, use a plunger. Dab some petroleum jelly around the edges of the plunger. This will ensure that the plunger seals tightly around the drain.

If the drain is still plugged, the next step is to use an auger or "snake." You can make a snake from an old wire coat hanger, by straightening out the hanger. Feed the snake into the drain by pushing and twisting it down. If this doesn't clear the drain, call a plumber.

## DINGY BATHTUB

Scrub the tub with a paste made of hydrogen peroxide and cream of tartar.

### DIRT ON BRICK WALLS

Brush off as much dirt as you can. Soak the bricks well with water, then scrub them with a solution of 1/4 cup (50 ml) of dishwasher detergent to one gallon (1 L) of water.

### WEEDS IN YOUR DRIVEWAY

Pour full-strength bleach on weeds along the cracks in sidewalks. They'll soon wither away.

### UNWANTED ANIMALS ON YOUR LAWN

Mix:
1 oz. cayenne pepper
1.5 oz. powdered mustard
2.5 oz. flour
Sprinkle this near the house. Cats and dogs will stay away. It's great for flower beds too.

# NUTRITION AND COOKING
## CANADA'S GUIDELINES FOR HEALTHY EATING

In order for us to stay healthy we need to eat a lot of different kinds of food. Canada's Guidelines for Healthy Eating recommends:

- Enjoy a variety of foods.
- Include cereals, breads, other grain products, vegetables and fruits.
- Choose low-fat dairy products, lean meats and foods prepared with little or no fat. Whole milk is good for pre-school children and it should also be used for making infant formula.
- Achieve and keep a healthy body weight by enjoying regular physical activity and healthy eating.
- Limit salt, alcohol and caffeine.

The Canada Food Guide divides all the foods we eat into four groups. Make sure you eat some foods from each group every day. This guide is being updated, and a new Food Guide will be available in 1992. If you would like a copy, contact your nearest Alberta Agriculture office.

*BAKING MADE EASY*

If you've decided to bake a cake, why not double the recipe and bake two? Freeze the second one.

*PREPARE-AHEAD PIE CRUST*

Roll out your pastry and cut it into circles. Freeze these between layers of plastic wrap or wax paper. When you need a pie crust, you can thaw one out quickly.

*STRETCH YOUR MEAT*

Cut down on the amount of meat you add to casseroles, sauces and soups.

*EGGS, EGGS, EGGS*

Your best cake recipe needs four eggs. You only have three. Do you have corn starch? You can replace four eggs with three eggs plus one tsp. (5 mL) of corn starch.

*FRIDGE ODOURS*

Keep an open box of baking soda in your fridge. It soaks up odours.

*SOUP STRAINING*

The cookbook says to strain the soup stock, but you don't have a strainer with holes small enough to do the job. Try putting a coffee filter in the strainer. It works like a charm.

*KIDDIE POP*

Do your kids love pop? Do you hate to give them so much sugar? Then make your own pop. Add 1/3 glass of club soda to 2/3 glass of fruit juice.

*HAVE YOU RUN OUT OF BAKING POWDER?*

You can make your own.
Mix:
2 tsp. of cream of tartar
1 tsp. of baking soda
1 tsp. of corn starch.
If you use this right away, you may leave out the starch.

# KITCHEN SHORTCUTS
## RECIPE LANGUAGE

| | |
|---|---|
| tbsp. | tablespoon |
| tsp. | teaspoon |
| oz. | ounce |
| liq. | liquid |
| lb. | pound (=16 ounces) |
| qt. | quart (=2 pints) |
| pt. | pint (=2 cups) |
| mL | millilitre |
| L | litre |
| kg | kilogram |

Some cookbooks use metric measurements. You can buy metric measuring cups and spoons almost everywhere. If you don't have metric measures, here is a chart which will help you to convert from imperial to metric.

| | |
|---|---|
| 1 tsp. | 5 mL |
| 1 cup | 250 mL |
| 2.2 lbs. | 1 kg |
| 1 tbsp. | 15 mL |
| 1 oz. | 30 g |

# YOUR NUTRITION TIPS

# CARING FOR YOUR CLOTHES
## SEWING TIPS

*KEEPING ZIPPERS UP*

If you have a zipper on a pair of pants or a skirt which doesn't want to stay up, here is a quick fix. Sew a small button near the top of the zipper. Then loop thread through the hole in the zipper pull. Now zip up. Loop the thread over the button. No more creeping zippers!

*IT'S A SNAP*

How do you position snaps for sewing? Try this: sew the small half on first. Now rub chalk on the little point. Lay the top fabric on it. The chalk marks the exact spot for the top half of the snap.

*LOOSE BUTTONS*

No time to sew a loose button? Dab the thread with clear nail polish. It will hold nicely.

*LETTING THE HEM DOWN ON JEANS*

Now you have a white line from the old hem. Get your child's crayons. Match a colour to the jeans. Now colour in the line. Iron your work. No more telltale line.

*STORE THOSE BUTTONS*

Egg cartons are great for this. Sizes and colours stay separate in each compartment.

*KEEP KNITTING NEEDLES HANDY*

Save your empty foil boxes. They are great for holding knitting needles and crochet hooks.

## LAUNDRY HINTS

*LINE DRYING IN WINTER*

It is freezing outside. Yet you want to hang your wash out. Add 1/2 cup of salt to the rinse water in the washing machine.

*KEEP CURTAINS CRISP*

Renew the crisp look of your curtains. Add 1/2 cup of powdered milk to the last rinse water.

*WHITE SNEAKERS*

Spray starch on new sneakers before you wear them. Dirt will wash right off. Re-spray after each washing.

*FABRIC SOFTENER*

Instead of liquid fabric softener, add 1/2 cup of white vinegar to the rinse water. It's cheaper, works just as well, and it's better for the environment.

*WATER TEMPERATURE*

Make sure you use the right temperature water for your washing. Clothing manufacturers in Canada always put "care" labels in their garments. Symbols are sometimes used on these labels. As a general rule, use hot water for white cottons, diapers and items are sometimes used on these labels. As a general rule, use hot water for white cottons, diapers and items which are very dirty. Warm water can be used on delicate fabrics and synthetic blends. Use cold water for dark colours, bright colours, washable woollens and lightly soiled items.

### SOAP OR DETERGENT?

Many people don't know the difference between soap and detergent. Soap is made by combining fats or oils in an alkaline base. Laundry soap usually has extra alkaline salts and chemical "builders" to make it work better. Soaps are very gentle on fabrics and skin, but they don't work to well in hard water. If your water is hard, soap can sometimes make your clothes appear dingy and gray.

Detergent is made from a variety of chemicals. It includes a surfactant, which is the main cleaning compound. It works well in hard water. Some of the best ingredients for detergent in hard water are phosphates. Phosphates clean well, but they are harmful to the environment. Many detergent brands have replaced phosphates with other chemicals which are safer for the environment and clean just as well.

### DETERGENT BOOSTER

Add a couple of capfuls of ammonia to your wash. Your clothes will be brighter. Ammonia is also environmentally friendly.

### ZIPPERS AND FASTENERS

Close all zippers, buttons and hooks, and turn pockets inside out, before washing.

# YOU AND YOUR ENVIRONMENT

The environment is the world we live in. It's important that we take care of it. We don't get a second chance! There are a lot of things we can do to make sure we don't do any more damage to the world around us. Here are some things you can do:

• Start a compost pile of kitchen scraps. Place scraps and grass clippings in a wooden box in your back yard. Stir the compost and wet it down with a hose every once in a while. After a few months you will have good fertilizer for your vegetable or flower garden.

• Recycle your newspapers. Put your old newspapers into a newspaper recycling bin.

• Use two sides of paper for writing. The back sides of junk mail make excellent drawing paper for kids. Ruse old envelopes for shopping lists.

• If you live in a community which has a recycling program, follow it.

• Instead of using air freshener sprays, place pretty dishes of "potpourri" in your bathroom and kitchen. "Potpourri" is a mixture of all kinds of nice smelling herbs and flowers which have been dried. You can buy packages of potpourri in drug stores and gift stores.

• Try to use fewer disposable items: paper towels, paper napkins, paper plates, foam cups, cotton swabs, and cotton balls.

• Turn off the water when you brush your teeth.

• Run the dishwasher only when it is full.

• If you change your own car oil, don't just dump the used oil in the garbage. Take it to an oil recycling centre. If you don't know where to take your old oil, call your local garage or mechanic for advice. Check with your local government to find out if there is a toxic waste "round-up" in your community. In many communities, toxic wastes are collected once a year and disposed of safely. If there isn't one in your community, why not start one?

• Plant a tree in your yard. Plants and trees help make our air quality better.

• Recycle your children's lunch bags, or pack your children's lunches in reusable lunch bags or boxes.

• Re-use your plastic grocery bags. Some grocery stores even give you a few cents per bag when you bring them in and use them again. Better yet, buy some canvas bags which you can use over and over again.

• Ovens use the most electricity of all of the appliances in your home. Try to use the oven for more than one thing at a time. Try cooking a roast and potatoes at the same time, or cook a casserole and a cake at the same time.

• Use an electric kettle rather than heating a kettle on the stove.

• Try taking the bus, walking or riding your bicycle to places that you used to drive to.

• Instead of just throwing a container out, try to think of another use for it. For example, will that empty coffee can hold pencils and pens? Can you use that empty egg carton to hold golf balls or buttons?

• Save gift wrap, ribbons, twist ties, and rubber bands. Try wrapping your gifts in colourful comics pages.

• Repair broken items instead of throwing them out.

• Always turn water taps off tightly. If they are leaking, get them fixed.

• Place aerators and water flow reducers on your taps and shower heads.

• Short showers use less water than baths. When you shower, turn off the water while you are shampooing and soaping. Them rinse off quickly.

• For more information about the environment contact:

**Alberta Environment Network**
**10511 Saskatchewan Drive**
**Edmonton, AB**
**T6E 4S1**
**(403) 433-9302**

# YOUR ENVIRONMENTAL TIPS

# REFERENCES

Here is a list of reference books. Ideas from these reference books are the backbone of this book. Each of these references has more references listed in it.

*Alternatives in Diapering.* This booklet is available at your public health unit,
**or**
send your name, address, and $1 for postage to *Alternatives in Diapering*, Distribution, c/o 5015 48 St., Camrose, AB T4V 3G3.

*The Canadian Green Consumer Guide.* Prepared by the Pollution Probe Foundation. McClelland & Stewart Inc. Toronto: 1989.

Gregg, Elizabeth M. and Boston Children's Medical Centre. *What To Do When There's Nothing To Do.* Delacorte Press. New York: 1968.

Johnson, Gordon K. *Environmental Tips: How You Can Save This Planet.* Detselig Enterprises, Ltd. Calgary, AB: 1990

Mitchell, Harris. *1200 Household Hints You Wanted To Know.* Southstar Publishers Ltd. Toronto: 1982.

*Our Fragile Future: A Southam Environment Project.* Southam Newspapers. October 7, 1989.
Stevenson, R.P. and Roy Doty. *Almanac For Home Owners.* Harper and Row. New York: 1972.

Swezey, K.M. and R. Scharff. *Formulas, Methods, Tips and Data for Home and Workshop*. Harper and Row. New York: 1979.

Walker, Georgiana. *The Celebration Book: Fun Things To Do With Your Family All Year Round*. G/L Publications. Glendale, CA: 1971.

The publications of:
Alberta Agriculture, Home Economics Branch
Alberta Transportation
Canadian Western Natural Gas
Consumer and Corporate Affairs
Health and Welfare Canada
Nortwestern Utilities
TransAlta Utilities

# OTHER TITLES IN THE
# PINE CANDLE ADULT NEW READER'S SERIES

Each book in this series covers a subject of interest to adult readers,
and is written in a style that makes it easy to read.

## ALBERTA HIGHLIGHTS
**ISBN 1-55105-004-8**
Take a tour of some of the most interesting spots in Alberta.

## NIGHT SKIES
**ISBN 1-55105-007-2**
Learn about the stars and planets while improving your reading.

## HOCKEY: CANADA'S NATIONAL GAME
**ISBN 1-55105-005-6**
The history of professional and amateur hockey in Canada.

## SOUPED UP
**ISBN 1-55105-009-9**
Ethnic recipes plus stories from new readers.

## RODEO WEST
**ISBN 1-55105-008-0**
Discover the rough-and-tumble rodeo circuit — and the people who live it.

Softcover          5.5 x 8.5          64 pages          $6.95 each

*Lone Pine Publishing* & *Alberta Association for Adult Literacy*
hope to carry on the tradition of the
**1990 Literacy Year**
with these excellent educational publications.

Buy these and other Lone Pine books from your local bookstore or
order directly from
*Lone Pine Publishing*
206,10426 - 81 Avenue, Edmonton, Alberta, T6E 1X5,
Phone: (403) 433-9333 Fax: (403) 433 9646